Opposite: *Open Door/Closed Door,* 1974–1975

Emerson's Parlor, 2005

THE McKNIGHT FOUNDATION

First Bridge, 1968
White Bear Lake, Minnesota (destroyed)

Introduction

The sculptor Siah Armajani is a citizen of the world. A native of Iran whose highly regarded work resides in public spaces and museum collections all over the globe, Armajani creates art that reflects his lifelong engagement with writers and thinkers from a wide range of countries and eras. His work also reflects his sincere desire for his fellow citizens to engage as well—with art, with democratic ideals, and with one another.

Armajani might be a citizen of the world, but he's also a 50-year resident of Minnesota. While he could live and work nearly anywhere, he has chosen to make the Twin Cities his home. Actually, Minnesota was chosen *for* him first: when Armajani was a young man, his father informed him that he'd soon be leaving his native Tehran to study at Macalester College in St. Paul. But after he earned his degree in philosophy, Armajani rented a studio in Minneapolis and went to work. He's been working here ever since—first on paintings and conceptual art, later on bridges and public spaces, and most recently on more inward-looking sculptures that meditate on democracy, war, iconic thinkers, and mortality.

One of Armajani's intellectual heroes, Ralph Waldo Emerson, characterized the authentic American scholar as "one who raises himself from private considerations, and breathes and lives on public and illustrious thoughts. He is the world's eye. He is the world's heart." All of this is true of Armajani, an artist remarkably free of ego who has long trained his eye and his heart on some of the most important questions we face as fellow Americans and fellow citizens of the world. We Minnesotans are immeasurably lucky that Siah Armajani chose our state as the place where he would read, think, and create the astonishing works that have for 50 years so captivated us and the rest of the world.

ROBERT J. STRUYK | Chair, The McKnight Foundation

Contents

An Exile Dreaming of Saint Adorno, 2009
Minneapolis Institute of Arts

Artist's Statement

What I wanted to write has been written by many others. The alchemy of my work comes from the base metal of others.

"Art does not express ideology but produces it as an object, makes it visible."
—Louis Althusser

"We have to rethink what the political function of culture would be in a situation where everything is cultural."
—Fredric Jameson

"I have always been
—Pablo Picasso

"There is a picture by Voltaire of despair—the total despair of a shipwrecked man who is swimming in the waves and struggling and squirming for his life when he receives the message that this ocean in which he finds himself does not have a shore..."—Ernst Bloch

SIAH ARMAJANI

"Why do they prefer to see people as 'unshaped matter, formless, unstructured, incompetent?'" —Noam Chomsky

"Are we perhaps here to
say: house, bridge, fountain,
gate, pitcher, fruit tree,
window,—at best: pillar,
tower...."
—Rainer Maria Rilke

an exile."

"It is part of morality not to be
at home in one's home."
—Theodor Adorno

"Culture is detectable geographically and the idea
of region should be understood as a term of value."
—John Dewey

Prayer, 1962
Walker Art Center, Minneapolis

First Bridge, 1968
White Bear Lake, Minnesota (destroyed)

Cellar Door, 1979
Weatherspoon Art Gallery,
University of North Carolina, Greensboro

Lissitzky's Neighborhood: Center House, 1978
Solomon R. Guggenheim Museum, New York, New York

Meeting Garden, 1980
Artpark, Lewiston, New York

Reading Garden #3, 1980
State University of New York at Purchase

We Have Never Been Modern

by Ian Bourland

In October of 2009 I was making my rounds in New York's Chelsea district, on assignment for *Artforum International*. My editor suggested that I stop by the reliably cosmopolitan and cutting-edge gallery Max Protetch and report back on a small installation by one of its artists, a reputed Persian sculptor whose name was oddly familiar. During my rambles through Chelsea, I see art that runs the gamut— the good, the bad, and the ugly—and am rarely surprised by what I see. But on that autumn day, in the small side gallery, I was entranced. Siah Armajani's most recent piece, a massive glass vitrine bedecked with the green, white, and red of the Iranian flag, clad in black metal, and crowned by a wounded figure cascading to her death, was like nothing I had ever seen. All the parts were familiar: the national symbolism, the references to modernist architecture and minimalist sculpture, the renderings of Spanish artist Goya's *Disasters of War* prints from the early 1800s that surrounded the sculpture. All these parts made sense to my critical brain, but their combination here was something entirely new.

That installation, *Murder in Tehran*, was Armajani's response to the violence that surrounded Mahmoud Ahmadinejad's contested 2009 election as Iran's president and the brutal police crackdown that followed. The woman atop the sculpture, whose limbs are cast and entombed within, is Neda Agha-Soltan, a young protester killed by a sniper during the outpouring of popular outrage at what is widely considered a rigged election. During this bloody decade, I have seen a lot of art that deals with the current array of global conflicts, much of it in vibrant Technicolor that mirrors our televised access to every corner of the globe. Unlike much of this work, which can feel like reportage, Armajani's sculpture was unmistakably art—beautiful, balanced, singular. But it also told me something about a specific time and place. I had read the news coverage of the Iranian election and its wake, but until I saw *Murder in Tehran*, I had not understood its visceral terror, its tragic parody of democracy, or the harrowing efficiency of its violence. What we see on CNN can be simultaneously, paradoxically intimate and alien, but with this work, Armajani reminds us that Neda could be someone we know, and that murder and corruption are part of our collective history. There but for the grace of God go we. But for the grace of God and our continued commitment to democracy, that is.

I wrote about *Murder in Tehran* twice in the ensuing months, and dragged anyone who would listen back to the gallery to see what I was talking about. Someone pointed out that Armajani had other large works nearby, in Staten Island and upstate at the Storm King Art Center in Mountainville. This is typical: one can find examples of Armajani's work scattered across the globe in places that range from the densest cities to the most picturesque countryside. And while each of these pieces is distinctive, mirroring its site as well as the aesthetic and political ideals Armajani has forged over half a century, the works are never flashy, never dominate the viewer or the environment. Instead, they speak to their viewers and environments and invite them to speak to one another.

Storm King is a rambling forest preserve punctuated with massive sculptures and serpentine earthworks. Some of the finest sculptors of the past century have work on permanent display here, and many of the pieces dominate the horizon with their monumental size. While these exercises in proportion and sublimity are exhilarating, it is easy to feel dwarfed by the environment. Armajani's piece, *Gazebo for Two Anarchists: Gabriella Antolini and Alberto Antolini* (1992), named for two Italian-American anarchists imprisoned during the Red Scare of 1919, offers a subtle counterpoint. Although constructed of steel and cut at hard angles, *Gazebo* offers a sense of openness and human-scale moderation. It nearly catches the viewer unaware as it comes into view at the bottom of a gentle slope.

The sculpture resembles an open boxcar, or a white bridge between two blue-gray towers. It is one of only two pieces at Storm King that allow viewers to enter and interact with the work. Indeed, the sculpture, which spans a constructed waterway, is incomplete without such participation. Once inside, you see that each of two "rooms" contains one chair facing across the corridor. The symbolism here is clear: two sitters, friends or foes, surrounded by open, luminescent walls and invited to converse, disagree, or collaborate on equal footing. The setup is a perfect analogy for what a democratic public sphere is supposed to do: create room for a diverse citizenry to engage on common ground, and create community through the act of communication. *Gazebo* not only reminds us of this process but also acts upon our bodies, teaching us what to do even as it allows a sense of freedom and play. But as inviting as the *Gazebo* may be, these seats are not comfortable: they are physically rigid and demand seriousness from the sitter. It is a lovely place to do the careful work of rational communication, but it exemplifies a quote Armajani loves from his favorite thinker, the German cultural critic and philosopher Theodor Adorno:

"It is part of morality not to be at home in one's home."

This latter point is important. Armajani's is an art that suspects and roots out complacency. He points out that we can never be comfortable with the world we have: our national vision demands that we constantly investigate the present and enact a better future. In spite of honoring sometimes-violent anarchists, Armajani's work does not condone violence, but rather summons the spirit of insurrection, action, and a more fully realized American ideal. The sculpture honors the turbulent history by which the nation was forged and constructs Armajani's vision of what that process entailed. *Gazebo* commemorates and renews the power of communication, equality, and collaboration that can span (in this case quite literally) our various national fault lines. Neither pop art nor art for art's sake, *Gazebo* hopes to teach us and to articulate for us the bridge between art and life, between ourselves and others. And yet, it is unmistakably still art: whimsical, sculptural, chromatically lovely, and like no other sitting room I've ever experienced. *Gazebo* is a memorial to the dead in the traditional sense, but also a reminder that there is still a future to be built—not just by artists and politicians but by us. We citizens, too, must build.

This may sound like pretty lofty stuff. It's all well and good to contemplate the communicative public sphere when one is hanging out in the rarefied space of an art gallery or seminar room, but what about real life? The convergence of art and daily life is one that Armajani doggedly pursues. His work has been, for most of his career, public. One of the finest examples is familiar to anyone who has spent time in the Twin Cities: the *Irene Hixon Whitney Bridge*, constructed in 1988 and spanning Interstate 94 between the Walker Art Center and Loring Park in Minneapolis. The bridge is a large-scale version of *Gazebo*, down to its blue-steel terminals and soft-yellow span and its literal bridging of two previously divided points—the art-filled sculpture garden and the city itself. The bridge also asks the viewer to become a participant, to cross the chaotic freeway below, and to feel and to move in a visceral way, even as the steel and timber of the structure create a safe environment for this passage to unfold. Armajani demands not only that we look, but also that we act, and he gives us the tools to do so.

It is fitting that a concise expression of Armajani's aims and means occupies such a prominent place in the life of the cities in which he has lived for 50 years. His work engages people the world over, but Armajani has elected to remain in the Twin Cities. This is the place to which his family sent him to escape the Shah's puppet regime, into the safekeeping of both his uncle Yahya (a familiar face to generations of students at Macalester College in St. Paul, where he was a professor of history) and a metropolis that has a history of protecting exiles like Hmong and Somalis who may never return to their homes but might find something else in the plains of the Middle West. Away from the exigencies and dissonances of the global art capitals, Armajani and his work have been nourished by the interdependence, the community, and the populism that are hallmarks of Minnesota's history and of his practice. While Armajani has built many bridges, houses, and reading rooms over the years, the crux of these many projects is there, captured in the bridge at Loring Park.

Armajani's bridge is not the most iconic work in the sculpture garden. Its other celebrated sculpture, *Spoonbridge and Cherry* (1985–1988) by Pop artists Claes Oldenburg and Coosje van Bruggen, is a reminder that art can delight and enliven us. No one would mistake that enormous utensil for anything but sculpture. But Armajani approaches us from a different pole of modern art—the long dialogue of modernism. To understand the ways in which Armajani has considered and adapted ideas whose roots extend from the Enlightenment through the evolution of modernism, we need to take a trip back into history and a few turns around the globe.

Art historians point to the work of a handful of Parisian painters in the mid-19th century as the dawn of modern art. Gustave Courbet, followed by Manet and his contemporaries 10 and 20 years later, developed an artistic practice marked by two primary emphases. First, they moved away from realism (the recent invention of the camera had freed art from its purely mimetic duties) and toward investigations of light, perception, and the two-dimensional, optical nature of painting. And they elevated formerly "profane" subject matter, from courtesans and absinthe drinkers to country laborers and bourgeois weekenders.

This art was modern because it specified a new role for artists, who were no longer beholden to traditional power centers like the church or the state but were instead agents in a rapidly expanding free market of producers and consumers in the industrializing West. Their work both depicted the daily life of this modernity (as opposed to radiant saints, great philosophers, or angelic nudes) and allowed the artist to investigate the properties specific to painting and sculpture themselves. Shorn of obligations to realism and traditional subject matter, the modern artist was free to

Louis Kahn Lecture Room, 1982
Fleisher Art Memorial, Philadelphia

Closet Under Dormer, 1984–85
Walker Art Center, Minneapolis

Closet Under Stairs, 1985
Hirshhorn Museum and Sculpture Garden,
Smithsonian Institution, Washington D.C.

Elements #11, 1987
Ludwig Museum, Cologne, Germany

Humphrey Garden, 1988
Hubert H. Humphrey Institute of Public Affairs
University of Minnesota, Minneapolis

SkyBridge #1, 1988
Minneapolis

make (and make a living from) what the era's great poet, Charles Baudelaire, extolled as *l'art pour l'art*—art for art's sake. This period just after the great upheavals of 1848, the Paris Commune, and the emergence of anarchism and Marxist economic analysis, also gave birth to a political avant-garde that frequently overlapped the artistic one. At the same time that modern art became connected to the commercial market by "an umbilical cord of gold," to quote the critic Clement Greenberg, it was also called on to promote a revolutionary politics. Of course this was a sometimes contradictory proposition, and a far cry from the artist's previous role as portraitist, embellisher of churches, or constructor of monuments.

This shift was theorized by Enlightenment philosopher Immanuel Kant, who argued for faith in what we can perceive concretely and for our ability to enlighten ourselves through a continuing process of rigorous questioning and self-evaluation. Such enlightened citizens look not to an external guide (whether a priest or a prince), but to their own analysis and judgment. In this view, art becomes an end unto itself—a sphere of human activity imbued with its own values and principles. For Kant's countryman G.W.F. Hegel, the development of individuals, political systems, and artwork was driven by a system of dialectics in which one position (thesis) is confronted with its opposite (antithesis) and the two resolve in a new position (synthesis). This was the engine, Hegel said, that drove human activity forward. Art, then, becomes both a historical artifact and evidence of the dialectic of history unfolding. This freed modern artists to be not only specialists in their own realms of economic activity, but also participants in the forward rush of modernity that upended all that came before.

What does all this have to do with Siah Armajani?

He certainly would have been familiar with this Continental, idealist tradition, educated as he was in German philosophy while a young man attending a Presbyterian missionary school in Iran. While at Macalester, Armajani was a self-admittedly poor student of art history, preferring his own investigations to the rote memorization of names and dates. He did, however, gravitate toward the work of the Constructivists, a group of artists in Leninist Russia who advocated the sameness of artist and citizen and the capacity for rationality and technology to bring about a better future—one in which art could function in the service of politics.

Constructivism was one form in a wide array of early 20th-century avant-garde circles that took up the duality of modern art practice: balancing social function with artmaking that pursues the problems specific to art itself. Armajani later honored the Constructivist El Lissitzky in a large installation on the first floor of the Guggenheim Museum. *Lissitzky's Neighborhood: Center House* (1977–1978) was a human-scale deconstruction and recasting of Constructivist tropes like clean lines, boldly hued geometric planes, horizontality, and function over ornamentation.

Throughout Armajani's career, he has investigated both the artist's embeddedness in society and the role of art as an applied practice rather than a rarefied commodity. Although *Lissitzky's Neighborhood* is one of the more literal invocations of this modernist tradition, modernism is also evident in the very materiality of Armajani's work. From his covered skyways in Minneapolis and Leipzig to his series of enclosed "reading rooms" to his most recent pieces, a series of tombs for thinkers who have been his intellectual beacons, Armajani continually reapplies glass and steel—the building blocks of modern architecture—in unadorned, geometric variations. One cannot help but draw associations between Armajani's structures and the "New Architecture" pioneered by the Bauhaus (a workshop based in Weimar-era Germany that cross-pollinated with the Constructivists), the wide array of then-contemporary avant-garde movements, and the populist regional architecture emerging from the American plains.

Bauhaus pioneers like Walter Gropius and Ludwig Mies van der Rohe attempted to apply both social progressivism and artistic principles to the development of comprehensive designs for functional buildings—not just the materials of the buildings themselves, but also the furniture, paintings, and housewares within. Glass and steel permitted the Bauhaus to achieve both a machine aesthetic that broke with earlier tradition and a sense of functional concision. The effect was an approach to building that was not only structurally sound, but solidly democratic in its transparency and openness and its rejection of epic façades and neoclassical ornamentation. Armajani says that he was influenced by *Glass Architecture*, a 1914 work by Paul Scheerbart arguing that architects could fundamentally reshape culture by altering its built environment. In particular, Scheerbart favored an architecture reliant on glass, which could be colored for aesthetic effect but would create a structure of literal openness. By eliminating the "closed character" of our environments, Scheerbart argued, architects could overturn tradition and uplift society. This balance of beauty (through light and color) and political engagement (through spaces that eradicate social distinction) reverberates through virtually all of Armajani's work during the past three decades. Just as the General Mills *Covered Walkway* (1990) in Minneapolis creates safe passage and aesthetic harmony with the environment with stunning economy of means (all white metal and angled glass), *Murder in Tehran* uses the closed form of the vitrine and blackout curtains to convey closure, inaccessibility, and the occlusions of an autocratic regime. The same materials and architectural vocabulary are used to distinct physical and psychological effect.

When Armajani began making art full time and teaching at the Minneapolis College of Art and Design in 1968, his contemporaries were making art that was utterly rarefied—pictures and sculptures that were about art itself and easily saleable to the highest bidder. The Constructivist dream had been subordinated to Stalinist social realism, and the New Architecture of the Bauhaus had been redirected into an International Style that stood for superficial modernity, eradicating local culture and truly usable public space. (Think of *Mad Men*, the TV show that depicts soft-bellied admen inhabiting glass and steel skyscrapers, surrounded by Abstract Expressionist paintings as they dream up ways to force products on a pliant public.)

What was Armajani to make of all this? The answer rested in a pair of essays by Theodor Adorno. Amid the aftermath of World War II and the advent of the postwar consumer economy, Adorno wrote a series of incisive essays that deeply influenced Armajani. "The Culture Industry: Enlightenment as Mass Deception," written with Max Horkheimer in 1944, presciently outlines the way in which the "culture industry" ruthlessly repackages political dissent into just another commodity, and suggests that the trappings of modern life are not indicators of a genuinely modern consciousness—quite the opposite. And the 1962 essay "Commitment" spells out the dangers of well-meaning political art: Jean-Paul Sartre's "committed art" was little more than a dressed-up intellectual exercise, while Bertolt Brecht's "didactic theater" sacrificed ideological clarity to theatrical needs.

The solution, according to Adorno, is to concede that all art is embedded in the social and is thereby political, but must also function, above all, as art. Both essays ring clear in Armajani's own work, which seems to insist that although we live in the most affluent of societies, we all still have miles to travel. Although Armajani could show us endless lovely images of bridges and reading rooms, to be truly political we must engage in a dialectic of our own with the work and its environment. We must cross those bridges, sit inside those reading rooms.

While Adorno, a witness to the horrors of fascism and totalitarianism, was skeptical of the Enlightenment's promise, his successors (like Jürgen Habermas) were more sanguine, postulating that rational communication in the public sphere could indeed guide us toward something better, toward our becoming truly modern. I would count Armajani among this more hopeful younger generation, marrying as he does the vision of the avant-garde with the materials of modernist architecture and the progressive spirit of communications theory. His art is one of decided engagement and cautious optimism. Of course, Armajani has a secret weapon that his European forebears did not: a voracious appetite for his adopted homeland. If the sometimes abstruse ideas above sound familiar, it may be because the ideals of progress through democracy, equality, and rationality are all embedded in the fabric of America's identity. The Founding Fathers shared the intellectual terrain of the European idealists, and our revolution was a shot that echoed from Latin America to Central Europe.

It was the truly American thinkers who continued to inspire Armajani with their possibility, openness, and pragmatism: Thomas Paine, Ralph Waldo Emerson, Walt Whitman, William James, and John Dewey are all writers whose work Armajani quotes repeatedly in his sculptures. As an immigrant, Armajani could dedicate himself to these thinkers and to making his own analysis of the American mythos with fresh eyes, rooting out the unique possibilities of our intellectual and social landscapes as well as our contradictions and shortcomings. Like Alexis de Tocqueville and countless other "outsider insiders," Armajani can see America clearly and draw from its reservoirs. Minneapolis gave him sanctuary, our thinkers gave him hope, and he in turn has given us some of our most graceful and most American public spaces.

This engagement has often unfolded in small-scale, intimate ways: rigorous studies of houses and domestic spaces like the deconstruction and re-imagining of Monticello in the *Thomas Jefferson House* (1976–1979) in Dayton, Ohio; or the modest, cozy reading cottage he constructed at Lake Placid, New York, for the 1980 Olympics. Look more closely at those wood, steel, and glass structures—they owe much to the vernacular architecture of the Midwest and its rail bridges, grain elevators, silos, and shipping containers, the networks of exchange and movement

that have connected the United States since the 19th century. There is a reverence
here for the quotidian architecture that we take for granted, and in which Armajani
locates the kernel of the American experience—not so dissimilar to the best impulses
of the European avant-garde, just played out on a different terrain.

What happened to the heroic painting, conceptual cleverness, and strident
declarations of "identity" that dominated the art world during most of Armajani's
career? He says that his reading and thinking made it clear to him that "[artists] can
be citizens with something to offer besides self-analysis. We can be part of society,
and not just a small élite supported by a wealthy minority." This spirit of careful,
humble engagement and subordination of ego to a greater openness and usefulness
to the public is manifest in the larger projects that grew out of Armajani's smaller
investigations during the 1970s. Armajani's noted *Covered Foot Bridge (Bridge over
a Nice Triangle Tree)* (1970) was a striking example of vernacular architecture built
horizontally, at a human scale, that deferred to its environment, whimsically curving
over a tree that grew below. This emphasis on both utility and the environment is
repeated in the Whitney Bridge, in the low, clean profile and inviting geometries
of the *Humphrey Garden* (1988) at the University of Minnesota, and in his
collaboration with public artist Scott Burton, landscape architect M. Paul Friedberg,
and architect Cesar Pelli to design the World Financial Center Plaza in Manhattan's
Battery Park City (1989). Armajani was particularly vocal in the latter project,
insisting that the massive urban redevelopment (built on infill from the construction
of the World Trade Center) be genuinely functional, sensitive to the changing
seasons, and unmarred by excess decoration or grand sculptural gestures.

But even as Armajani has dedicated his career to downplaying his own
artistic ego in favor of an open practice that coaxes the best from American
philosophical and architectural traditions, he is not uncritical. Quite the opposite, in
fact. His reverence is tempered by a continued skepticism. His
bridges, plazas, and reading rooms at once embrace and prod
their users, suggesting that none of what we have can be
taken for granted, and there is still—always—more work to
be done. We can never be at home in our homes. Perhaps this is
a unique perspective of the exile, a man who cannot, in the wake of the 1979 Iranian
revolution and the Ahmadinejad election, return to his first home, a place that lives

on in the aphorisms and poetry that dot both his sculptures and his speech. Who better to keep us honest, to look at America and her citizens with brutal clarity?

This is how we might best understand the past decade and last phase of Armajani's practice, one that has turned markedly from the lightness and openness of the 1980s and '90s to the darker, polemical, and closed surfaces of collapsed houses, memorials, and tombs. A piece like *Murder in Tehran* brings Armajani full circle: back to an art that has a different kind of social function than his earlier bridges and reading rooms, and back to a place that Armajani quit because, while it bore the trappings of modernity, its autocratic government would not permit the openness, communication, tolerance, and questioning that a citizenry needs to be truly modern. We all witness the reverberations today, in Neda's murder and in the debate at the time of this writing about whether a woman will be brutally executed for adultery or humanely granted refuge in Europe.

In the face of such atrocity, Armajani can no longer play the part of the patient public artist—and after 50 years, he has earned at least that much. In *Fallujah* (2004–2005), he applied glass, steel, and the form of the domicile to give a human face and scale to a concrete event (the battle in that Iraqi city) that saturated American news but whose importance was lost on many viewers. *Fallujah* and *Murder in Tehran* are similar in their dark palettes, closed forms, and emphasis on discrete historical events, in contrast to the openness and participatory elements of Armajani's earlier work. These two pieces are also similar in message: in Tehran as in Baghdad, a failure of democracy is a failure of modernity. Modernity cannot be built like so many Burger Kings but must be allowed to flourish from within, in the hearts and minds of a free citizenry. In Armajani's account, the true evil—that of modernity silenced—is a real prospect on both sides of the Atlantic. Our history is no bulwark against the future, and the viability of the American idea rests in all citizens' hands.

Why do I keep coming back to Armajani's work? It has something I rarely see on my walks around Chelsea: generosity. Armajani's art is fiercely theoretical, but in his quest to engage he never succumbs to mere diatribe. At the same time, the work never contents itself with simple elegance, never devolves into clichés about the "plight of the exile," never includes details of Armajani's remarkable life. This is not art for art's sake, nor is it an exercise in identity politics. It is rigorous, unflinching art that sparks dialogue and pushes the dialectic of modernism to its promised but yet-unfulfilled conclusion.

The art world might have moved on, but you can find Siah Armajani still in Minneapolis. He's there, quietly working, making art for and about us, showing us how we can keep moving, keep talking, keep questioning once he is no longer here to show us the way. What he calls the "last phase" of his work consists of tombs for his intellectual heroes, and, ultimately, for himself. This is both elegiac and fitting in the last stage of a career dedicated to making our American project accessible, useful, and vibrant.

—

Ian Bourland is a New York–based art historian and critic who is completing his Ph.D. in art history at the University of Chicago and travels frequently to Minnesota. He writes about issues of identity, nation, and globalization in contemporary art; his writing has appeared most recently in Artforum, The Economist, and Canvas.

World Financial Center Plaza, 1989
New York, New York
(Collaboration with Scott Burton,
Cesar Pelli, M. Paul Friedberg)

Elements #18, 1988
Museum für Moderne Kunst,
Frankfurt, Germany

Elements #35, 1989
Museum of Modern Art,
New York, New York

*Sacco and Vanzetti Reading
Room No. 3*, 1991
Museum für Moderne Kunst,
Frankfurt, Germany

Crossings

by Darsie Alexander

Siah Armajani is often referred to as a public artist. As a generalization, this one is defensible. Over his long career, Armajani's hybrid art, which falls somewhere between sculpture and architecture, has attracted an international audience of pedestrians and onlookers drawn to the visible locations his work occupies—over roadways, in urban parks, and between buildings. But for a good many years, he has called Minnesota home—studying here, working here, and marrying here. He has produced some of the most memorable city landmarks in Minneapolis, including a downtown skyway and an elegant, almost otherworldly, footbridge over the 16-lane torrent of urban traffic that constitutes Interstate 94 and Hennepin/Lyndale avenues. The *Irene Hixon Whitney Bridge* must be Minnesota's most public of public-art fixtures, within eyeshot of some 155,000 drivers who pass daily, not to mention the cautious pedestrians who cross a safe distance overhead.

The Minnesotan home base seems aptly suited to the kind of art Armajani makes—the wide expanse of Midwestern landscape (to traverse), the intense weather (to escape), and the long vistas (to take in or interrupt). The blue of the Whitney Bridge is, without question, the blue of the background sky at certain times of year, against which its lines fade and flicker. It is within this place, geographically removed from art-world epicenters such as New York and Los Angeles, that his practice has emerged to world acclaim—a serious and quiet practice whose presence is woven into the fabric of the layered cultural landscape of the Twin Cities, one that includes writers, performers, artists, craftspeople, and filmmakers, among other notable makers and thinkers. Amid these colleagues and compatriots Armajani's voice is singular and fluid, capable of moving from philosophy to literature to art to politics to poetry and back again. Like so many conversations between people and ideas, his often remain private. Yet communication through words occupies a privileged place in his art: "It is fair to be crossing, to have crossed," reads a line from the John Ashbery poem that Armajani commissioned for his bridge.

Armajani's work, like language, can bring people together, yet it does not require his presence. Often using wood or metal, the artist's distinctive aesthetic has become readily identifiable, possessing an elemental and rigorously architectonic formal order and inward discipline that is easily recognized from a distance. Yet his work, which ranges from freestanding sculptures to benches, pavilions, and bridges, is designed not only for visual reception but also for intimate human expressions such as reading, walking, and thinking—actions that we undertake every day in different ways. He makes space for others to occupy, never demanding that they engage in prescribed behaviors or interactions. Do you greet the person across from you? Lose yourself in thought when you read? Prefer to sit in the shade? The openness presented by his work is meant for the individual, whose singular identity shapes personal reaction—to sit or not, like or dislike, cross or stay put. What Armajani's art acknowledges is a certain kind of personal freedom, a freedom that is a subtle text to his works. This doesn't translate into overtly political or patriotic gestures but into offerings for others to seize or react to. Some of these offerings can be found in Minnesota, where the public constitutes the artist's eventual collaborator; they are the people rushing across his skyway to work, or sitting for lunch in his Loring Park gazebo. These individuals may or may not know Armajani's name, as renowned a force as he is in the spheres of local and international art. They can nevertheless feel his presence and experience his unparalleled vision in the places they cross and inhabit.

—

Since 2008, Darsie Alexander has been chief curator at the Walker Art Center in Minneapolis, where she oversees exhibitions, visual arts, design, performing arts, film/video, and Minneapolis Sculpture Garden programs. She was previously senior curator at the Baltimore Museum of Art and an assistant curator at the Museum of Modern Art in New York City, and has written extensively on performance art, conceptualism, and new media.

Siah Armajani: Citizen Artist
by Dennis Szakacs

> As long as art is the beauty parlor of civilization, neither art nor civilization is secure.
> —John Dewey

Siah Armajani's radical reformation of the purpose of art in a democratic society is one of the most ambitious and sustained projects undertaken in American art since the 1960s. And the story of his career over the last 40 years reflects the major changes that have taken place in contemporary art and American culture during this period. Dewey's famous admonition, used by Armajani in several early works, seems more alarming than ever as the relentless art market merges with seductive reality television to push artists and museums into ever more glamorous yet far less secure territory.

Since his early 20s, Armajani has lived in Minnesota, far from the global capitals of culture, but close to the heart of his subject: a humble and direct engagement with ideals of public life and civic responsibility. His sculpture and public projects (bridges, gardens, and reading rooms) are inspired by Midwestern vernacular architecture, frequently incorporate quotations from American literary figures such as Ralph Waldo Emerson, Walt Whitman, Robert Frost, Wallace Stevens, John Ashbery, and Frank O'Hara, and are often dedicated to historical figures ranging from Thomas Paine and Noam Chomsky to Sacco and Vanzetti. His works are for the most part functional and rigorous, designed to encourage contemplation, discussion, and debate, and are informed as much by his early engagement with conceptual art as by the ancient Persian architecture and miniatures he experienced during his childhood in Iran. Armajani was a hybrid before the word become fashionable, and his work to this day is an intriguing and altogether original amalgamation of ancient and modern, Western and Eastern, global and local, public and private.

Armajani had achieved international success by the end of the 1980s, with works included in the shows Documenta 8 and Skulptur Projekte Münster 87, a major survey exhibition at the Stedelijk Museum, the completion of the *Irene Hixon Whitney Bridge* in Minneapolis, and his collaboration with Scott Burton, Cesar Pelli, and M. Paul Friedberg on the celebrated World Financial Center Plaza in New York's Battery Park City. He had put into exceptional practice the theoretical positions of his *Manifesto: Public Sculpture in the Context of American Democracy*, a call to replace artistic self-expression with functional works that serve a civic purpose. Armajani compiled this major statement between 1968 and 1978 and revised it in 1993.

These achievements led to an unprecedented and ultimately life-changing commission to design a torch-and-bridge structure for the 1996 Summer Olympics in Atlanta, a project that put the work of a living artist in front of the nearly 40 million television viewers who watched Muhammad Ali light the cauldron, but in the end was so mismanaged that Armajani was forced to disown it. Although his design was praised by major critics outside Atlanta, it never became the city's Eiffel Tower, which its steel latticework construction recalled. Perhaps it did not have the time to fully enter the consciousness of the city, in the way that often happens when bold new forms are first rejected and then later embraced by the public. The Atlanta Braves baseball team, which took over the stadium after the Olympics, disliked the structure so much that they moved it to the edge of a parking lot, where it remains today unused and abandoned, a sad symbol for what could have been a triumphal moment for contemporary art in America.

Atlanta's pivotal role in Armajani's career may be viewed within the larger context of the privatization of public space, which has only grown since then, due in large part to governmental policies that increasingly place corporate interests over those of the common good. At the same time (and perhaps as a result), artists who take more activist and socially engaged positions have fewer opportunities to realize major public commissions than those whose interests and concerns reflect our more entertainment-driven reality. Armajani's work has little in common with the current taste for public-art projects, which are by and large either mammoth pop spectacles or ephemeral interactions, usually presented in regularly programmed, privately owned spaces, and almost always temporary and fleeting.

After nearly 30 years of high-profile public projects in America and Europe, the experience of Atlanta led Armajani ultimately to reject his *Manifesto*, to enter into a more than decade-long withdrawal from regular exhibitions and commissions, and to reformulate his work. As Armajani was working on how to proceed, he must have looked back to his series of works from the late 1980s devoted to American anarchists. Four *Sacco and Vanzetti Reading Rooms*, based on the infamous trials and execution of the two Italian immigrants in 1927, as well as a series of gazebos dedicated to other anarchists of the era, recalled the cages in which the anarchists were tried and marked a darker turn that has become even more pronounced in his studio works of the last decade.

The anarchist series was Armajani's most in-depth examination of a specific subject and was an extended meditation on the limits of personal liberty within American democracy. For Armajani, the anarchists represent the contradictions and polarities within the American political system that are debated, discussed, and adjudicated, yet never fully resolved. The series is especially prescient in light of post-9/11 America: Sacco and Vanzetti were victims of the country's first "war on terror," and the jingoism, erosion of individual rights, distrust of immigrants, and isolationism that defined American policy then are still reverberating now.

It was from these reading rooms and gazebos that Armajani found the way to the next great phase of his career. The cagelike structures of that series developed into ever more sophisticated containers for theatrical set pieces; in 2000, Armajani began building a series of nearly full-scale rooms of glass, his first extensive use of that material. Works like *Glass Room for an Exile* (2002), *Fallujah* (2004–2005), and *Poe's Study* (2008) directly embrace Armajani's own story as an immigrant, respond to the turbulence within the region where he was born, and confront the fears and anxieties that come with age.

As Armajani was becoming more personal, as he was beginning to reveal more of himself, he was also pushing the viewer out, and the change from largely public concerns to private ones required a change in architecture as well. These recent works, containing simple beds, tables, chairs, and highly symbolic objects relating to the particular subject of the room, draw inspiration from Giacometti's *Palace at 4 a.m.* (1932), a work that Armajani says has haunted him for 40 years. Rather than designing spaces for public use and making installations that people could enter, he is now moving toward completely enclosed spaces that seal off the viewer physically yet allow total visual access from the outside. "Since 1968 my work had been public, useful, and open, and in 2000 it turned personal and melancholy," Armajani said recently. "I had tried for years to hide it and fight against it, but I failed, so now the work is closed." And yet, out of what Armajani has characterized as failure has emerged a vital new direction in the work of a profound and prolific artist.

—

Dennis Szakacs is the director of the Orange County Museum of Art (OCMA) in Newport Beach, California, and has also worked in New York City at the New Museum of Contemporary Art and P.S. 1. With the Walker Art Center in Minneapolis, he is co-organizing a Siah Armajani exhibition slated to open at OCMA in the fall of 2013 and travel to the Walker in 2014.

Fallujah: The Commitment of the Artist

by María Dolores Jiménez-Blanco

Between the 18th and 19th centuries, at the dawn of the modern era, the French painter Jacques-Louis David (1748–1825) and the Spanish painter Francisco de Goya (1746–1828) established a new status for the artist. Both painters thought their work should satisfy human needs that were more important than mere aesthetic delight, and each decided to go beyond the usual interpretations of history and drama to create images that represented the social and political concerns of his fellow patriots.

After David and Goya came another Spanish artist, Pablo Picasso (1881–1973), who has often been called a modern hero *par excellence.* If Picasso was not the most radical artist of his time—perhaps he was the last of the great old masters rather than the first master of the new era—he was still the undisputed champion of freedom in art.

Pablo Picasso, *Guernica*
1937

That focus was not limited to the formal aspects of his creativity. Picasso's most famous piece might be *Guernica*, the painting he created in 1937 after the bombing of the Basque city by Nazi planes supporting Franco's Nationalist forces during the Spanish Civil War. In May of 1937, while painting *Guernica* and still in shock from the images of the city's destruction he had seen in Paris newspapers, Picasso declared:

The Spanish struggle is the fight of reaction against the people, against freedom. My whole life as an artist has been nothing more than a continuous struggle against reaction and the death of art. . . . In the panel on which I am working which I shall call *Guernica*, and in all my recent works of art, I clearly express my abhorrence of the military caste which has sunk Spain in an ocean of pain and death. . . .

Guernica soon became an icon that represents every fight against injustice and every crime committed in the cause of war. As such, the work has transcended the actual incident that inspired its creation.

So has Armajani's *Fallujah*, to which Picasso's words could apply with very little alteration. *Fallujah* was Armajani's response to a specific and very painful episode of the second Gulf War: the bloody 2004 assault on the Iraqi city of Fallujah by U.S.-led forces targeting insurgents who had taken cover in residential areas. Hundreds of Iraqi civilians were killed and more than 200,000 fled their ruined homes.

Numerous visual allusions underline the dialogue between Armajani's *Fallujah* and Picasso's *Guernica*: the hanging lightbulb within the burning eye/ sun shape, the flames, the presence of a horse (which Armajani transforms into a wooden rocking horse) in the chaos of a bombed house. But Armajani also finds a more poetic way to quote Picasso. Just as Picasso did with a flower emerging from the hand of a soldier, Armajani preserves a hint of hope for the future—the purity of youth represented in his sculpture by the rocking horse, an element present from Armajani's very first model of the work.

Fallujah, 2004–05
Lannan Foundation, Santa Fe, New Mexico

Beyond its formal references to Picasso's *Guernica*, the piece stands as a moral tribute to the heritage of all those artists who, like Picasso, and like David and Goya before him, have been sensitive to the human concerns of their time. Just like them, but very much on his own terms, Armajani has created an image of courage and despair that makes specific reference to a particular moment, but that also makes visible the turmoil of war and destruction wherever and whenever it might occur.

In April of 2007, two years after its completion, Armajani's *Fallujah* was shown at the Artium Museum of Contemporary Art in Vitoria, Spain, in an exhibition that coincided with the 70th anniversary of the bombing of nearby Guernica. Before then, no gallery or museum in America had been willing to show it. After two exhibitions in Spain, the piece was subsequently shown in the United States. By deciding not to remain quiet in the face of catastrophe and in the middle of a deafening worldwide silence, Armajani created with *Fallujah* a new emblem of the artist's commitment to social and political engagement.

—

María Dolores Jiménez-Blanco, a professor of art history at the Complutense University of Madrid, is the author of numerous studies of 20th-century art. She has worked for the Phillips Collection in Washington, D.C., and the Solomon R. Guggenheim Museum in New York City, and has curated exhibitions for institutions that include the Museo Nacional Centro de Arte Reina Sofia and Fundación MAPFRE.

Dictionary for Building

by Thierry Davila; translated from the French by Lisa Johns

By Siah Armajani's own admission, his *Dictionary for Building* represents "the most important chapter of [his] artistic life." One could say that it is a prerequisite for understanding his work and capturing the spirit behind it. Armajani began production on the collection in 1974, around the time that he made a decision to define himself as a public artist, thereby setting forth an explicit desire to move away from art exhibitions in the most traditional sense. This genuine treasure of forms is composed of different pieces of varying sizes (models, miniature models, large-scale structures, and other sculptural layouts)— constructions that are potentially destined to occupy public space or, more precisely, to enliven it.

The oldest part of the *Dictionary*, developed between 1974 and 1975, consists of 131 small-scale works and is housed today in the collection at Mamco in Geneva. It was around 1967 that Armajani began to show interest in architecture—that of bridges in particular, a form we see recurring in his work, but also in the vernacular of building practices, introducing into his work an opening of space, the rules that govern the functions of its properties, and new levels of visibility.

To create this first part of his *Dictionary*, Armajani crisscrossed the United States in a grand tradition of American culture (found in its literature and especially in its film). Spotting a striking geometric shape in one place, a one-of-a-kind building in another—all objects unique in their form and functionality—he rendered these structures into models, a kind of note-taking in three dimensions. He used simple materials like cardboard, string, and wood chips, which reflect modest constructions that he first discovered, then inventoried.

These inaugural works express the power of plasticity and the power of invention as evidenced by a construction lacking in distinctive characteristics, architecture, style, or authorship. They are "invisible" structures that Armajani helps to rescue from oblivion. His concerns include the creation of the most common architecture, one that is both a public good and a public object, and the fact that the simplest structures are often the least recognized. These structures are not personal, but they deserve to be the object of an archive of public space and history and heritage. The *Dictionary for Building* is a genuine catalog of works that possess virtues at once architectural and sculptural, that are also true testing grounds for constructions to come, that make up an archive of small pieces with the potential to communicate across time and through creations of the largest dimensions.

"Public sculpture rejects the idea of the universality of art," Armajani wrote in a manifesto that he composed between 1968 and 1978. The constructs cataloged in the *Dictionary for Building*—an authentic travelogue that journals the exploration of architectural and sculptural singularity—carry out Armajani's deconstruction of universality. The *Dictionary for Building* is a veritable manual for the singular use of public space.

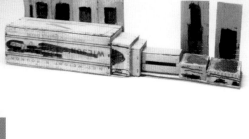

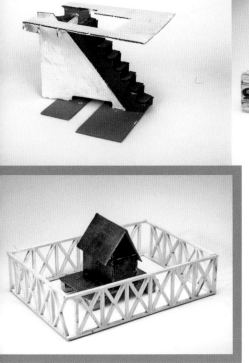

Dictionary for Building (131 models), 1974–75
Musée d'Art Moderne et Contemporain,
Geneva, Switzerland

Thierry Davila is the curator in charge of publications at the Musée d'Art Moderne et Contemporain (Mamco) in Geneva, Switzerland, and a lecturer in contemporary art at the University of Geneva. Mamco mounted retrospective exhibitions of Siah Armajani's work in 1995 and 2007.

Poetry Garden, 1992
Lannan Foundation, Los Angeles

*Gazebo For Two Anarchists:Gabriella Antolini
and Alberto Antonlini*, 1993
Storm King Park,
Mountainville, New York

Bridge, Tower, Cauldron, 1996
Centennial Olympics, Atlanta, Georgia

Beloit Fishing Bridge, 1997
Beloit, Wisconsin

Glass Room, 2000
Walker Art Center, Minneapolis

Post Office Pocket Park, 1996
Wayzata, Minnesota

Glass Bridge, 2003
Cheekwood Botanical Garden & Museum of Art,
Nashville, Tennessee

The Nobility of Usefulness

by Calvin Tomkins

In the early 1980s, the public art movement in America was in full flower. A lively group of mostly young and highly ambitious artists, fed up with the gallery system and its pressure to produce expensive trinkets for rich buyers, had turned to the public sphere, where recent changes in national and local government policies were making it possible for them to collaborate with architects, engineers, city planners, real-estate developers, and others in the design or re-design of parks, playgrounds, waterfronts, indoor and outdoor plazas, and other spaces that people could actually use and enjoy. I wanted to write about this surprising development, so I began asking around, and every artist I talked to told me I had to meet Siah Armajani, whose work and thinking were of central importance to all of them. "Siah has really brought about a significant mutation in what art is," said Scott Burton, a New York sculptor and performance artist whose sculptures functioned as high-concept chairs and tables. "It's profoundly American, what he's done, and, of course, he probably couldn't have done it if he'd been born here."

When I went out to Minneapolis to meet Siah, what struck me right away was his deep, joyous immersion in American culture and civilization. Like so many other immigrants who have helped to reveal and enhance our possibilities, Siah truly believes in the first principles of American democracy. Jefferson and Franklin, Emerson and Thoreau, Whitman and John Dewey are living presences in his life, so it was perfectly natural for him to embed their words in the bridges, reading rooms, and vernacular structures of his artistic practice. He has taught us a great deal about ourselves, about our past and, with luck, our future, and about what he once described as "the nobility of usefulness." It's a nice phrase, and I think it helps to describe his own immense contribution.

—

Calvin Tomkins has been a staff writer for The New Yorker *since 1960. He profiled Siah Armajani for the magazine in 1990; his other profile subjects have included Marcel Duchamp, Robert Rauschenberg, Philip Johnson, Frank Stella, Frank Gehry, Richard Serra, and Jasper Johns.*

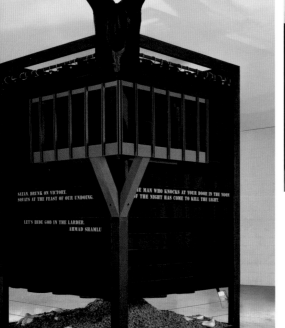

Lighthouse and Bridge, 1996
Staten Island, New York

Floating Poetry Room, 2005
Ijborg, Amsterdam, Netherlands

Murder In Tehran, 2009
Private collection

Front Porch For Walter Benjamin, 2000
Private collection

A Span of Poetry
by Eric Lorberer

It did not become a bridge until the first person walked across it.
—Siah Armajani

Over the years I've noticed how often this bridge is affectionately referred to as "the Ashbery Bridge" by poets and others, because of the site-specific text John Ashbery was commissioned to write for it. Visual-arts aficionados are more likely to dub it "Armajani's Bridge" after the acclaimed sculptor who so magnificently imagined it into being. In conversation, one almost never hears it called by its technically accurate name, the *Irene Hixon Whitney Bridge*, which honors the arts patron who helped fund it.

Irene Hixon Whitney Bridge, 1998, Minneapolis

AND NOW I CANNOT REMEMBER HOW I WOULD
HAVE HAD IT. IT IS NOT A CONDUIT (CONFLUENCE?)
BUT A PLACE. THE PLACE, OF MOVEMENT AND AN
ORDER: THE PLACE OF OLD ORDER. BUT THE TAIL
END OF THE MOVEMENT IS NEW. DRIVING US TO
SAY WHAT WE ARE THINKING. IT IS SO MUCH LIKE A
BEACH AFTER ALL, WHERE YOU STAND AND THINK
OF GOING NO FURTHER. AND IT IS GOOD WHEN
YOU GET TO NO FURTHER. IT IS LIKE A REASON
THAT PICKS YOU UP AND PLACES YOU WHERE YOU
ALWAYS WANTED TO BE. THIS FAR. IT IS FAIR TO BE
CROSSING, TO HAVE CROSSED. THEN THERE IS NO

PROMISE IN THE OTHER. HERE IT IS. STEEL AND AIR,
A MOTTLED PRESENCE, SMALL PANACEA AND LUCKY
FOR US. AND THEN IT GOT VERY COOL. —JOHN ASHBERY

I view it as a sign of the artwork's success that it's connected in so many viewers' minds with the poem by John Ashbery that adorns it. Armajani loves American literature—especially poetry—and often weaves it into his work: Robert Frost's "Mending Wall" in the poetry lounge at the California Institute of Technology; a wonderful passage from "Meditations in an Emergency" by Frank O'Hara ("I can't even enjoy a blade of grass unless I know there's a subway handy, or a record store or some other sign that people do not totally regret life") in the World Financial Center Plaza in Manhattan's Battery Park City; Wallace Stevens's "Anecdote of the Jar" in a garden at the Lannan Foundation in Santa Monica, California; and dozens more.

Armajani is justly lauded for the way his works offer the experience of the space as it unfolds to the viewer. Christian Bernard, director of the Musée d'Art Moderne et Contemporain in Geneva, has written that Armajani's works "only get their full and final meaning in their pragmatic articulation in public space." In this sense, the Ashbery Bridge is undoubtedly one of his finest accomplishments, bringing all the elements of form and content into exquisite alignment. It functions fully as a pedestrian bridge, allowing amblers safe and exhilarating passage over a staggering 16 lanes of motor-vehicle traffic, yet it is anything but pedestrian in its design. Significantly, it joins two public spaces—to the west, the Minneapolis Sculpture Garden, which contains works by Alexander Calder, Jacques Lipschitz, Dan Graham, Ellsworth Kelly, Jenny Holzer, Louise Bourgeois, Claes Oldenburg and Coosje van Bruggen, and many others; and to the east, Loring Park, which offers a splendid and necessary retreat from the downtown that sits just above it.

You might note that the two spaces the bridge connects represent the art world and the city, but it's important to mention that it was also created jointly by these two worlds. For those of us who believe that art has a role to play in civic life, that is cause for some joy: here is a massive piece of sculpture that was conceived by an artist of considerable grace, then constructed by workers from the local transportation authority. The finished work is both utilitarian and symbolic, both art object (at 375 feet long, it is the largest sculpture ever commissioned by the Walker Art Center) and practical conveyance for Minneapolis residents and visitors.

Armajani's design for the bridge ingeniously incorporates the three fundamental kinds of bridge structures. I read this as an attempt by this bridge-obsessed sculptor to create a kind of *ur*-bridge—to rhapsodize about the very *idea* of a bridge. At its core, the structure employs a sturdy steel truss design, with crossbeams in blue and yellow repeating across the whole horizontal of the bridge; the history of this workmanlike form is also nicely alluded to by the through-lines of the fir-plank floor and the dark-green railing, which offer an unobtrusive stability for the bridge's users. But Armajani dramatically also employs the form of the suspension bridge, starting in the yellow western portion and swooping down, and the form of the arch bridge in the eastern blue portion beyond that, resulting in a triumphantly overdesigned space that evokes classic architecture, 19th-century American industrial structure, and postmodernism all at once.

The collision of these forms creates a majestic enterprise. The two catenary arcs overlap at the bridge's center, metaphorically joining the worlds of art and city; it's also significant that the arcs are reverse images of each other,

creating a slightly askew mirror effect that the bridge design plays with throughout, and that Ashbery's poem also deploys powerfully. Finally, note how deftly Armajani has used color, choosing the highly recessive tones of light blue for the arch side of the bridge and pale yellow for the suspension side. These atmospheric shades evoke sun and sky and invite the natural world to participate in the material nature of the bridge; they also underscore the sense of transition from one side to the other, again creating an off-kilter symmetry that highlights the double dream at the heart of this unique project.

—

Eric Lorberer is a Minneapolis poet and the editor of Rain Taxi Review of Books, *an award-winning quarterly journal. This piece is excerpted from a talk originally given in 2006 at the conference "Some Trees in a Forest of Possibility" at the University of Massachusetts, Amherst. An essay version, published in the literary magazine* jubilat, *was named a Notable Essay in* Best American Essays 2008.

SIAH ARMAJANI: An Artist's Life

1939	Born in Tehran, Iran
1960	Leaves Tehran to enroll in Macalester College in St. Paul, where his uncle Yahya teaches history
1962	Has a black-and-white calligraphy painting exhibited at the Walker Art Center in Minneapolis (which subsequently purchases the piece for its permanent collection)
1963	Graduates from Macalester
1966	Marries Macalester classmate Barbara Bauer
1967	Becomes an American citizen
1968	Hired to teach at the Minneapolis College of Art and Design; builds *First Bridge* in White Bear Lake, Minnesota
1970	*A Number Between Zero and One* included in "Information," the first-ever museum show of conceptual art, at the Museum of Modern Art in New York, New York; *Covered Foot Bridge (Bridge over a Nice Triangle Tree)* included in "9 Artists/9 Spaces" at the Walker Art Center
1974	Begins work on *Dictionary for Building*, his "index of art and architectural possibilities"
1978	*Lissitzky's Neighborhood: Center House* included in "Young American Artists" exhibition at the Solomon R. Guggenheim Museum in New York, New York
1979	Builds *Reading House* in Lake Placid, New York, as a commission for the "Art at the Olympics" exhibition during the 1980 Winter Olympics
1981	*Dictionary for Building* exhibited at Max Protetch Gallery, New York, New York; commissions include *Office for Four*, Hudson River Museum, Yonkers, New York; *Employee Lounge*, Hirshhorn Museum, Washington, D.C.; and *NOAA Bridges*, Western Regional Center of the National Oceanographic and Atmospheric Administration, Seattle
1982	*Poetry Lounge* commissioned by the California Institute of Technology, Pasadena; *Louis Kahn Lecture Room* commissioned by the Fleisher Art Memorial, Philadelphia

1983   *NOAA Bridges* opens to the public

1985   "Siah Armajani: Bridges, Houses, Communal Spaces, *Dictionary for Building*" opens at the Institute of Contemporary Art at the University of Pennsylvania

1986   Begins collaborating with architect Cesar Pelli, fellow artist Scott Burton, and landscape architect M. Paul Friedberg on the World Financial Center Plaza at Battery Park City in New York, New York

1987   Solo exhibitions in Switzerland, Netherlands, Germany, and France include *Sacco and Vanzetti Reading Room No. 1*

1988   *Irene Hixon Whitney Bridge* opens in Minneapolis, as do *SkyBridge #1* and the *Humphrey Garden*

1989   Collaborates with Pelli on structures for the Yerba Buena Center office tower in San Francisco and the Norwest Center *(SkyBridge #1)* in Minneapolis; World Financial Center Plaza opens to the public

1990   Profiled by Calvin Tomkins in the March 19 issue of *The New Yorker*; *Sacco and Vanzetti Reading Room No. 4* shown at Hirshhorn Museum and Sculpture Garden, Washington, D.C.

1991   *Sacco and Vanzetti Reading Room No. 3* included in "20th Century Art" exhibition at Museum für Moderne Kunst, Frankfurt, Germany

1992   "*The Poetry Garden* and Recent Works" opens at the Lannan Foundation in Los Angeles

1995   Has solo show at the Musée d'Art Moderne et Contemporain (Mamco), Geneva

1996   Muhammad Ali lights the cauldron of the *Bridge, Tower, Cauldron* sculpture commissioned for the Summer Olympics in Atlanta

1998   *Room for Noam Chomsky: The Last Anarchist* installed at P.S. 1 in Long Island City, New York

2000   *Bridge for Iowa City* opens in Iowa City, Iowa

2003   Works that open to the public include *Bentley Plaza* at Ohio University, Athens, Ohio; *Glass Bridge* at the Cheekwood Botanical Garden & Museum of Art, Nashville, Tennessee; and *George Simmel Footbridge*, Strasbourg, France

2004   Included in "Gardens of Iran: Ancient Wisdom, New Visions" at the Tehran Museum of Contemporary Art

2005   *Floating Poetry Room* opens outside Amsterdam, Netherlands

2006   Included in "Word into Art: Artists of the Modern Middle East" at the British Museum in London; *The Chess Garden* opens in Des Moines, Iowa

2007   *Fallujah* is shown for the first time at the Artium de Alava, Vitoria-Gasteiz, Spain

2009   "Siah Armajani: *Murder in Tehran*" opens at Max Protetch Gallery

2010   *An Exile Dreaming of Saint Adorno* is acquired by the Minneapolis Institute of Arts after its appearance in the museum's "Until Now: Collecting the New (1960–2010)" exhibition

Selected Solo and Group Exhibitions

2010   Until Now: Collecting the New (1960–2010)
                Minneapolis Institute of Arts

2007   Siah Armajani
                Artium de Alava, Vitoria-Gasteiz, Spain
                Mamco, Geneva, Switzerland

2006   Word into Art: Artists of the Modern Middle East
                British Museum, London

2005   Siah Armajani
                Weinstein Gallery, Minneapolis

2004   Architecture and Arts: 1900–2000
                Palazzo Ducale, Genoa, Italy
        Gardens of Iran: Ancient Wisdom, New Visions
                Tehran Museum of Contemporary Art, Tehran, Iran

2002   Siah Armajani: *Glass Room for Walter Benjamin*
                Jiri Svestka Gallery, Prague, Czech Republic

2001   Art Unlimited: Art/32/Basel
                Basel, Switzerland

2000   Siah Armajani
                University of Iowa, Iowa City

1999   Siah Armajani
                Diputación Provincial de Huesca, Spain
                Fundación César Manrique, Canary Islands
                Museo Nacional Centro de Arte Reina Sofia, Madrid, Spain

1998   Siah Armajani: *Dictionary for Building*
                Matthew Architecture Gallery, University of Edinburgh, Scotland

1997   Views from Abroad: European Perspectives on American Art
                Museum für Moderne Kunst, Frankfurt, Germany

1996   Anarchistic Contributions
                Neue Galerie am Landesmuseum Joanneum, Graz, Austria
        Monument et modernité: État des lieux, commandes publiques en France, 1990–1996
                Musée du Luxembourg, Paris

Selected Solo and Group Exhibitions

1995   Siah Armajani
                Mamco, Geneva

1994   Siah Armajani, Sculpture and Public Art Projects
                Ikon Gallery, Birmingham, England

1993   Différentes Natures: Visions de l'Art Contemporain
                Place de la Défense, Paris
        Unpainted to the Last: *Moby-Dick* and Twentieth-Century American Art
                Spencer Museum of Art, University of Kansas, Lawrence

1992   Century of Sculpture
                Stedelijk Museum, Amsterdam
                Nieuwe Kerk, Amsterdam
        The Poetry Garden and Recent Works
                Lannan Foundation, Los Angeles

1991   20th Century Art
                Museum für Moderne Kunst
        Elements
                Max Protetch Gallery, New York, New York

1990   Culture and Commentary: An Eighties Perspective
                Hirshhorn Museum and Sculpture Garden, Smithsonian
                Institution, Washington, D.C.

1988   Carnegie International
                Carnegie Museum of Art, Pittsburgh
        View Points: Post-War Painting and Sculpture
                Solomon R. Guggenheim Museum, New York, New York

1987   Documenta 8
                Museum Fridericianum, Kassel, Germany
        Emerging Artists 1978–1986: Selections from the Exxon Series
                Solomon R. Guggenheim Museum
        Siah Armajani
                Galerie Rudolf Zwirner, Cologne, Germany
                Galerie Ghislaine-Hussenot, Paris
                Kunsthalle Basel, Switzerland
                Stedelijk Museum, Amsterdam
        Skulptur Projekte Münster 87
                Westfälisches Landesmuseum, Münster, Germany

Selected Solo and Group Exhibitions

1986   Bridges
            Cambridge Multicultural Arts Center, Cambridge, Massachusetts
      Second Sight: Biennial IV
            San Francisco Museum of Modern Art, California
      Sonsbeek 86
            Arnhem, Netherlands

1985   Siah Armajani: Bridges, Houses, Communal Spaces, *Dictionary for Building*
            Institute of Contemporary Art, University of Pennsylvania, Philadelphia

1984   Content: A Contemporary Focus, 1974–1984
            Hirshhorn Museum and Sculpture Garden
      Furniture, Furnishings: Subject and Object
            Museum of Art, Rhode Island School of Design, Providence
            Wesleyan University, Middletown, Connecticut
            Munson-Williams-Proctor Arts Institute, Utica, New York
            Berkshire Museum, Pittsfield, Massachusetts
            Vassar College, Poughkeepsie, New York
            Brattleboro Museum and Art Center, Brattleboro, Vermont
            Maryland Institute College of Art, Baltimore
      An International Survey of Recent Painting and Sculpture
            Museum of Modern Art, New York, New York

1983   Directions 1983
            Hirshhorn Museum and Sculpture Garden
      New Art
            The Tate Gallery, London

1982   Documenta 7
            Museum Fridericianum
      74th Annual American Exhibition
            Art Institute of Chicago

1981   Artists Gardens and Parks
            Hayden Gallery, Massachusetts Institute of Technology, Cambridge
            Museum of Contemporary Art, Chicago
      Biennial
            Whitney Museum of American Art, New York, New York
      Dictionary for Building I
            Max Protetch Gallery

Selected Solo and Group Exhibitions

1980   Drawings: The Pluralist Decade
        39th Venice Biennale, United States Pavilion, Venice, Italy
        Biblioteca Naciónal, Madrid, Spain
        Gulbenkian Museum, Lisbon, Portugal
        Henie-Onstad Art Centre, Oslo, Norway
        Institute of Contemporary Art, University of Pennsylvania
        Kunstforeningen, Copenhagen, Denmark
        Museum of Contemporary Art, Chicago

1979   *First Reading Room*
        Kansas City Art Institute, Kansas City, Missouri
        Max Protetch Gallery
        New Gallery of Contemporary Art, Cleveland

1978   Architectural Analogues
        Whitney Museum of American Art
   Documenta 6
        Museum Fridericianum
   Red School House for Thomas Paine
        Philadelphia College of Art, Philadelphia
   Young American Artists
        Solomon R. Guggenheim Museum

1977   16 Projects/4 Artists
        Wright State University, Dayton, Ohio
   Scale and Environment: 10 Sculptors
        Walker Art Center, Minneapolis

1976   Commissioned Video Works: *Skylight at Monticello*
        University Art Museum, Berkeley, California

1975   Sculpture for a New Era
        Federal Center, Chicago

1974   Discussions: Works/Words
        The Institute for Contemporary Art, Clocktower Gallery, New York, New York

1972   Operation Vesuvius
        Henry Gallery, University of Washington at Seattle
        Galleria d'Arte, II Centro, Naples, Italy

1971   Works for New Spaces
            Walker Art Center

1970   9 Artists/9 Spaces
            Minnesota State Arts Council, Minneapolis
        Art in the Mind
            Allen Art Museum, Oberlin College, Oberlin, Ohio
        Information
            Museum of Modern Art, New York

1969   Art by Telephone
            Museum of Contemporary Art, Chicago

Selected Sculptures
(denotes permanent sculptures)

2009   *An Exile Dreaming of Saint Adorno*, Minneapolis Institute of Arts

2006   *The Chess Garden*, Des Moines, Iowa

2005   *Floating Poetry Room*, Ijborg, Amsterdam, Netherlands

2003   *Bentley Plaza*, Ohio University, Athens, Ohio
        Glass Bridge, Cheekwood Botanical Garden and Museum of Art, Nashville, Tennessee
        George Simmel Footbridge, Strasbourg, France

2001   *Gazebo*, Village Shalom, Overland Park, Kansas
        Mural, The Sosland Foundation, Kansas City, Missouri

2000   *Bridge for Iowa City*, Iowa City, Iowa
        Gazebo with Picnic Table, Strasbourg
        Glass Room, Walker Art Center, Minneapolis
        Picnic Table for Huesca, Bielsa, Huesca, Spain

1999   *Lannan Poetry Garden #2*, Beloit College, Beloit, Wisconsin

1997   *Three Skyway Bridges for the City of Leipzig*, Leipzig, Germany
        Beloit Fishing Bridge, Beloit

1996   *Bridge, Tower, Cauldron*, 1996 Summer Olympics, Atlanta, Georgia
        The Lighthouse and Bridge, Staten Island, New York
        Post Office Pocket Park, Wayzata, Minnesota

Selected Sculptures
(denotes permanent sculptures)

1994 *Bridge/Ramp for the City of Stuttgart*, Stuttgart, Germany
Gazebo for the Irene Hixon Whitney Bridge, Minneapolis
Garden, Villa Arson Museum, Nice, France
Room for the First Anarchist Henry David Thoreau, Galerie der Stadt
  Esslingen, Esslingen, Germany

1993 *Gazebo for Two Anarchists: Gabriella Antolini and Alberto Antolini*, Storm
  King Art Center, Mountainville, New York

1990 *Sacco and Vanzetti Reading Room No. 4*, Hirshhorn Museum and Sculpture
  Garden, Smithsonian Institution, Washington, D.C.

1989 World Financial Center Plaza, New York, New York (collaboration with
  Scott Burton, Cesar Pelli, and M. Paul Friedberg)
SkyBridge #2, Minneapolis

1988 *Irene Hixon Whitney Bridge*, Minneapolis
SkyBridge #1, Minneapolis (collaboration with Cesar Pelli)
Humphrey Garden, Hubert H. Humphrey Institute of Public Affairs,
  University of Minnesota, Minneapolis

1987 *Poetry Garden*, Münster, Germany
Sacco and Vanzetti Reading Room No. 1, Kunsthalle, Basel

1983 *NOAA Bridges*, National Oceanic and Atmospheric Administration,
  Seattle, Washington

1982 *Poetry Lounge*, Baxter Art Gallery, California Institute of Technology, Pasadena
Louis Kahn Lecture Room, Fleisher Art Memorial, Philadelphia

1981 *Office for Four*, Hudson River Museum, Yonkers, New York

1978 *Lissitzky's Neighborhood: Center House*, Solomon R. Guggenheim Museum,
  New York, New York

1977 *Thomas Jefferson's House: West Wing, Sunset House*, Walker Art Center,
  Minneapolis

1972 *Sunset Bridge*, Stamford Township, Minnesota

1970 *Covered Foot Bridge (Bridge over a Nice Triangle Tree)*, Minneapolis

1968 *First Bridge*, White Bear Lake, Minnesota

McKnight Distinguished Artists

1998	Dominick Argento
1999	Warren MacKenzie
2000	Robert Bly
2001	Dale Warland
2002	Emilie Buchwald
2003	Mike Lynch
2004	Stanislaw Skrowaczewski
2005	Judy Onofrio
2006	Lou Bellamy
2007	Kinji Akagawa
2008	Bill Holm
2009	Bain Boehlke

About the Award

The Distinguished Artist Award recognizes artists who, like Siah Armajani, have chosen to make their lives and careers in Minnesota, thereby making our state a more culturally vibrant place. Although they had the talent and the opportunity to pursue their work elsewhere, these artists chose to stay—and by staying, they have made a difference. They have founded and strengthened arts organizations, inspired younger artists, attracted audiences and patrons. Best of all, they have made wonderful, thought-provoking art.

The award, which includes $50,000, goes to one Minnesota artist each year. Nominations are open to everyone, and those received by March 31 are considered the same year. The panel that selects the recipient is made up of five people who have longtime familiarity with the Minnesota arts community.

Our thanks go to panelists Philip Bither, Walker Art Center's senior curator of performing arts; Graydon Royce, theater critic at the Minneapolis *Star Tribune*; Stewart Turnquist, former coordinator of the Minnesota Artists Exhibition Program at the Minneapolis Institute of Arts; 2001 McKnight Distinguished Artist Dale Warland, founder of the Dale Warland Singers; and 2002 McKnight Distinguished Artist Emilie Buchwald, founder of Milkweed Editions. Their high standards and thoughtful consideration make this award a truly meaningful tribute to Minnesota's most influential artists.

VICKIE BENSON | Arts program director
The McKnight Foundation

Credits

frankhart, ink.-Colleen Frankhart | Editing
velvetpeel-Joanne Grobe | Design
Shapco | Printing | Certified PIM Great Printer Environmental Initiative

Siah Armajani is represented by Meulensteen Gallery, New York.

ABOUT THE MCKNIGHT FOUNDATION

The McKnight Foundation, a Minnesota-based family foundation, seeks to improve the quality of life for present and future generations. Through grantmaking, coalition-building, and encouragement of strategic policy reform, the Foundation uses its resources to attend, unite, and empower those it serves. Founded in 1953 and independently endowed by William and Maude McKnight, the foundation had assets of approximately $1.8 billion and granted about $98 million in 2009, of which about 10% was directed to support an environment in which artists are valued leaders in our community, with access to the resources and opportunities they need to succeed. In Minnesota, the Foundation also makes grants to support education and learning, our region and communities, and the environment.

The McKnight Foundation is committed to the protection of our environment, a philosophy that underlies our practice of using paper with postconsumer waste content and, wherever possible, environmentally friendly inks. Additionally, we partner with printers who participate in the PIM Great Printer Environmental Initiative. This book was printed with soy-based inks on recycled paper containing 30% postconsumer waste.

An Exile Dreaming of Saint Adorno, 2009
Minneapolis Institute of Arts